The Eclogues

by Virgil

Edited by Anthony Uyl

Devoted Publishing

Woodstock, Ontario, 2016

The Eclogues

37 BC

by Virgil

Edited by Anthony Uyl

Contact us at: devotedpub@hotmail.com
Visit us on Facebook: @DevotedPublishing
Get more print products via our website: www.devotedpublishing.com

Published in Woodstock, Ontario, Canada 2016.

For bulk educational rates, contact us at the email address above!

ISBN: 978-1-988297-43-9

Table of Contents

ECLOGUE I 5
ECLOGUE II 9
ECLOGUE III 11
ECLOGUE IV 15
ECLOGUE V 17
ECLOGUE VI 21
ECLOGUE VII 23
ECLOGUE VIII 27
ECLOGUE IX 31
ECLOGUE X 35

ECLOGUE I

MELIBOEUS, TITYRUS

MELIBOEUS
You, Tityrus, 'neath a broad beech-canopy
Reclining, on the slender oat rehearse
Your silvan ditties: I from my sweet fields,
And home's familiar bounds, even now depart.
Exiled from home am I; while, Tityrus, you
Sit careless in the shade, and, at your call,
"Fair Amaryllis" bid the woods resound.

TITYRUS
O Meliboeus, 'twas a god vouchsafed
This ease to us, for him a god will I
Deem ever, and from my folds a tender lamb
Oft with its life-blood shall his altar stain.
His gift it is that, as your eyes may see,
My kine may roam at large, and I myself
Play on my shepherd's pipe what songs I will.

MELIBOEUS
I grudge you not the boon, but marvel more,
Such wide confusion fills the country-side.
See, sick at heart I drive my she-goats on,
And this one, O my Tityrus, scarce can lead:
For 'mid the hazel-thicket here but now
She dropped her new-yeaned twins on the bare flint,
Hope of the flock- an ill, I mind me well,
Which many a time, but for my blinded sense,
The thunder-stricken oak foretold, oft too
From hollow trunk the raven's ominous cry.
But who this god of yours? Come, Tityrus, tell.

TITYRUS
The city, Meliboeus, they call Rome,
I, simpleton, deemed like this town of ours,
Whereto we shepherds oft are wont to drive
The younglings of the flock: so too I knew
Whelps to resemble dogs, and kids their dams,
Comparing small with great; but this as far
Above all other cities rears her head
As cypress above pliant osier towers.

MELIBOEUS
And what so potent cause took you to Rome?

TITYRUS

Freedom, which, though belated, cast at length
Her eyes upon the sluggard, when my beard
'Gan whiter fall beneath the barber's blade-
Cast eyes, I say, and, though long tarrying, came,
Now when, from Galatea's yoke released,
I serve but Amaryllis: for I will own,
While Galatea reigned over me, I had
No hope of freedom, and no thought to save.
Though many a victim from my folds went forth,
Or rich cheese pressed for the unthankful town,
Never with laden hands returned I home.

MELIBOEUS

I used to wonder, Amaryllis, why
You cried to heaven so sadly, and for whom
You left the apples hanging on the trees;
'Twas Tityrus was away. Why, Tityrus,
The very pines, the very water-springs,
The very vineyards, cried aloud for you.

TITYRUS

What could I do? how else from bonds be freed,
Or otherwhere find gods so nigh to aid?
There, Meliboeus, I saw that youth to whom
Yearly for twice six days my altars smoke.
There instant answer gave he to my suit,
"Feed, as before, your kine, boys, rear your bulls."

MELIBOEUS

So in old age, you happy man, your fields
Will still be yours, and ample for your need!
Though, with bare stones o'erspread, the pastures all
Be choked with rushy mire, your ewes with young
By no strange fodder will be tried, nor hurt
Through taint contagious of a neighbouring flock.
Happy old man, who 'mid familiar streams
And hallowed springs, will court the cooling shade!
Here, as of old, your neighbour's bordering hedge,
That feasts with willow-flower the Hybla bees,
Shall oft with gentle murmur lull to sleep,
While the leaf-dresser beneath some tall rock
Uplifts his song, nor cease their cooings hoarse
The wood-pigeons that are your heart's delight,
Nor doves their moaning in the elm-tree top.

TITYRUS

Sooner shall light stags, therefore, feed in air,
The seas their fish leave naked on the strand,
Germans and Parthians shift their natural bounds,
And these the Arar, those the Tigris drink,
Than from my heart his face and memory fade.

MELIBOEUS
But we far hence, to burning Libya some,
Some to the Scythian steppes, or thy swift flood,
Cretan Oaxes, now must wend our way,
Or Britain, from the whole world sundered far.
Ah! shall I ever in aftertime behold
My native bounds- see many a harvest hence
With ravished eyes the lowly turf-roofed cot
Where I was king? These fallows, trimmed so fair,
Some brutal soldier will possess these fields
An alien master. Ah! to what a pass
Has civil discord brought our hapless folk!
For such as these, then, were our furrows sown!
Now, Meliboeus, graft your pears, now set
Your vines in order! Go, once happy flock,
My she-goats, go. Never again shall I,
Stretched in green cave, behold you from afar
Hang from the bushy rock; my songs are sung;
Never again will you, with me to tend,
On clover-flower, or bitter willows, browse.

TITYRUS
Yet here, this night, you might repose with me,
On green leaves pillowed: apples ripe have I,
Soft chestnuts, and of curdled milk enow.
And, see, the farm-roof chimneys smoke afar,
And from the hills the shadows lengthening fall!

ECLOGUE II

ALEXIS

The shepherd Corydon with love was fired
For fair Alexis, his own master's joy:
No room for hope had he, yet, none the less,
The thick-leaved shadowy-soaring beech-tree grove
Still would he haunt, and there alone, as thus,
To woods and hills pour forth his artless strains.
"Cruel Alexis, heed you naught my songs?
Have you no pity? you'll drive me to my death.
Now even the cattle court the cooling shade
And the green lizard hides him in the thorn:
Now for tired mowers, with the fierce heat spent,
Pounds Thestilis her mess of savoury herbs,
Wild thyme and garlic. I, with none beside,
Save hoarse cicalas shrilling through the brake,
Still track your footprints 'neath the broiling sun.
Better have borne the petulant proud disdain
Of Amaryllis, or Menalcas wooed,
Albeit he was so dark, and you so fair!
Trust not too much to colour, beauteous boy;
White privets fall, dark hyacinths are culled.
You scorn me, Alexis, who or what I am
Care not to ask- how rich in flocks, or how
In snow-white milk abounding: yet for me
Roam on Sicilian hills a thousand lambs;
Summer or winter, still my milk-pails brim.
I sing as erst Amphion of Circe sang,
What time he went to call his cattle home
On Attic Aracynthus. Nor am I
So ill to look on: lately on the beach
I saw myself, when winds had stilled the sea,
And, if that mirror lie not, would not fear
Daphnis to challenge, though yourself were judge.
Ah! were you but content with me to dwell,
Some lowly cot in the rough fields our home,
Shoot down the stags, or with green osier-wand
Round up the straggling flock! There you with me
In silvan strains will learn to rival Pan.
Pan first with wax taught reed with reed to join;
For sheep alike and shepherd Pan hath care.
Nor with the reed's edge fear you to make rough
Your dainty lip; such arts as these to learn
What did Amyntas do?- what did he not?
A pipe have I, of hemlock-stalks compact
In lessening lengths, Damoetas' dying-gift:
'Mine once,' quoth he, 'now yours, as heir to own.'
Foolish Amyntas heard and envied me.
Ay, and two fawns, I risked my neck to find
In a steep glen, with coats white-dappled still,
From a sheep's udders suckled twice a day-
These still I keep for you; which Thestilis

Implores me oft to let her lead away;
And she shall have them, since my gifts you spurn.
Come hither, beauteous boy; for you the Nymphs
Bring baskets, see, with lilies brimmed; for you,
Plucking pale violets and poppy-heads,
Now the fair Naiad, of narcissus flower
And fragrant fennel, doth one posy twine-
With cassia then, and other scented herbs,
Blends them, and sets the tender hyacinth off
With yellow marigold. I too will pick
Quinces all silvered-o'er with hoary down,
Chestnuts, which Amaryllis wont to love,
And waxen plums withal: this fruit no less
Shall have its meed of honour; and I will pluck
You too, ye laurels, and you, ye myrtles, near,
For so your sweets ye mingle. Corydon,
You are a boor, nor heeds a whit your gifts
Alexis; no, nor would Iollas yield,
Should gifts decide the day. Alack! alack!
What misery have I brought upon my head!-
Loosed on the flowers Siroces to my bane,
And the wild boar upon my crystal springs!
Whom do you fly, infatuate? gods ere now,
And Dardan Paris, have made the woods their home.
Let Pallas keep the towers her hand hath built,
Us before all things let the woods delight.
The grim-eyed lioness pursues the wolf,
The wolf the she-goat, the she-goat herself
In wanton sport the flowering cytisus,
And Corydon Alexis, each led on
By their own longing. See, the ox comes home
With plough up-tilted, and the shadows grow
To twice their length with the departing sun,
Yet me love burns, for who can limit love?
Ah! Corydon, Corydon, what hath crazed your wit?
Your vine half-pruned hangs on the leafy elm;
Why haste you not to weave what need requires
Of pliant rush or osier? Scorned by this,
Elsewhere some new Alexis you will find."

ECLOGUE III

MENALCAS, DAMOETAS, PALAEMON

MENALCAS
Who owns the flock, Damoetas? Meliboeus?

DAMOETAS
Nay, they are Aegon's sheep, of late by him
Committed to my care.

MENALCAS
O every way
Unhappy sheep, unhappy flock! while he
Still courts Neaera, fearing lest her choice
Should fall on me, this hireling shepherd here
Wrings hourly twice their udders, from the flock
Filching the life-juice, from the lambs their milk.

DAMOETAS
Hold! not so ready with your jeers at men!
We know who once, and in what shrine with you-
The he-goats looked aside- the light nymphs laughed-

MENALCAS
Ay, then, I warrant, when they saw me slash
Micon's young vines and trees with spiteful hook.

DAMOETAS
Or here by these old beeches, when you broke
The bow and arrows of Damon; for you chafed
When first you saw them given to the boy,
Cross-grained Menalcas, ay, and had you not
Done him some mischief, would have chafed to death.

MENALCAS
With thieves so daring, what can masters do?
Did I not see you, rogue, in ambush lie
For Damon's goat, while loud Lycisca barked?
And when I cried, "Where is he off to now?
Gather your flock together, Tityrus,"
You hid behind the sedges.

DAMOETAS
Well, was he
Whom I had conquered still to keep the goat.
Which in the piping-match my pipe had won!
You may not know it, but the goat was mine.

MENALCAS
You out-pipe him? when had you ever pipe
Wax-welded? in the cross-ways used you not
On grating straw some miserable tune
To mangle?

DAMOETAS

Well, then, shall we try our skill
Each against each in turn? Lest you be loth,
I pledge this heifer; every day she comes
Twice to the milking-pail, and feeds withal
Two young ones at her udder: say you now
What you will stake upon the match with me.

MENALCAS

Naught from the flock I'll venture, for at home
I have a father and a step-dame harsh,
And twice a day both reckon up the flock,
And one withal the kids. But I will stake,
Seeing you are so mad, what you yourself
Will own more priceless far- two beechen cups
By the divine art of Alcimedon
Wrought and embossed, whereon a limber vine,
Wreathed round them by the graver's facile tool,
Twines over clustering ivy-berries pale.
Two figures, one Conon, in the midst he set,
And one- how call you him, who with his wand
Marked out for all men the whole round of heaven,
That they who reap, or stoop behind the plough,
Might know their several seasons? Nor as yet
Have I set lip to them, but lay them by.

DAMOETAS

For me too wrought the same Alcimedon
A pair of cups, and round the handles wreathed
Pliant acanthus, Orpheus in the midst,
The forests following in his wake; nor yet
Have I set lip to them, but lay them by.
Matched with a heifer, who would prate of cups?

MENALCAS

You shall not balk me now; where'er you bid,
I shall be with you; only let us have
For auditor- or see, to serve our turn,
Yonder Palaemon comes! In singing-bouts
I'll see you play the challenger no more.

DAMOETAS

Out then with what you have; I shall not shrink,
Nor budge for any man: only do you,
Neighbour Palaemon, with your whole heart's skill-
For it is no slight matter-play your part.

PALAEMON

Say on then, since on the greensward we sit,
And now is burgeoning both field and tree;
Now is the forest green, and now the year
At fairest. Do you first, Damoetas, sing,
Then you, Menalcas, in alternate strain:
Alternate strains are to the Muses dear.

DAMOETAS

"From Jove the Muse began; Jove filleth all,
Makes the earth fruitful, for my songs hath care."

MENALCAS

"Me Phoebus loves; for Phoebus his own gifts,
Bays and sweet-blushing hyacinths, I keep."

DAMOETAS
"Gay Galatea throws an apple at me,
Then hies to the willows, hoping to be seen."

MENALCAS
"My dear Amyntas comes unasked to me;
Not Delia to my dogs is better known."

DAMOETAS
"Gifts for my love I've found; mine eyes have marked
Where the wood-pigeons build their airy nests."

MENALCAS
"Ten golden apples have I sent my boy,
All that I could, to-morrow as many more."

DAMOETAS
"What words to me, and uttered O how oft,
Hath Galatea spoke! waft some of them,
Ye winds, I pray you, for the gods to hear."

MENALCAS
"It profiteth me naught, Amyntas mine,
That in your very heart you spurn me not,
If, while you hunt the boar, I guard the nets."

DAMOETAS
"Prithee, Iollas, for my birthday guest
Send me your Phyllis; when for the young crops
I slay my heifer, you yourself shall come."

MENALCAS
"I am all hers; she wept to see me go,
And, lingering on the word, 'farewell' she said,
'My beautiful Iollas, fare you well.'"

DAMOETAS
"Fell as the wolf is to the folded flock,
Rain to ripe corn, Sirocco to the trees,
The wrath of Amaryllis is to me."

MENALCAS
"As moisture to the corn, to ewes with young
Lithe willow, as arbute to the yeanling kids,
So sweet Amyntas, and none else, to me."

DAMOETAS
"My Muse, although she be but country-bred,
Is loved by Pollio: O Pierian Maids,
Pray you, a heifer for your reader feed!"

MENALCAS
"Pollio himself too doth new verses make:
Feed ye a bull now ripe to butt with horn,
And scatter with his hooves the flying sand."

DAMOETAS
"Who loves thee, Pollio, may he thither come
Where thee he joys beholding; ay, for him
Let honey flow, the thorn-bush spices bear."

MENALCAS
"Who hates not Bavius, let him also love
Thy songs, O Maevius, ay, and therewithal
Yoke foxes to his car, and he-goats milk."

DAMOETAS
"You, picking flowers and strawberries that grow
So near the ground, fly hence, boys, get you gone!
There's a cold adder lurking in the grass."

MENALCAS
"Forbear, my sheep, to tread too near the brink;
Yon bank is ill to trust to; even now
The ram himself, see, dries his dripping fleece!"

DAMOETAS
"Back with the she-goats, Tityrus, grazing there
So near the river! I, when time shall serve,
Will take them all, and wash them in the pool."

MENALCAS
"Boys, get your sheep together; if the heat,
As late it did, forestall us with the milk,
Vainly the dried-up udders shall we wring."

DAMOETAS
"How lean my bull amid the fattening vetch!
Alack! alack! for herdsman and for herd!
It is the self-same love that wastes us both."

MENALCAS
"These truly- nor is even love the cause-
Scarce have the flesh to keep their bones together
Some evil eye my lambkins hath bewitched."

DAMOETAS
"Say in what clime- and you shall be withal
My great Apollo- the whole breadth of heaven
Opens no wider than three ells to view."

MENALCAS
"Say in what country grow such flowers as bear
The names of kings upon their petals writ,
And you shall have fair Phyllis for your own."

PALAEMON
Not mine betwixt such rivals to decide:
You well deserve the heifer, so does he,
With all who either fear the sweets of love,
Or taste its bitterness. Now, boys, shut off
The sluices, for the fields have drunk their fill.

ECLOGUE IV

POLLIO

Muses of Sicily, essay we now
A somewhat loftier task! Not all men love
Coppice or lowly tamarisk: sing we woods,
Woods worthy of a Consul let them be.

Now the last age by Cumae's Sibyl sung
Has come and gone, and the majestic roll
Of circling centuries begins anew:
Justice returns, returns old Saturn's reign,
With a new breed of men sent down from heaven.
Only do thou, at the boy's birth in whom
The iron shall cease, the golden race arise,
Befriend him, chaste Lucina; 'tis thine own
Apollo reigns. And in thy consulate,
This glorious age, O Pollio, shall begin,
And the months enter on their mighty march.
Under thy guidance, whatso tracks remain
Of our old wickedness, once done away,
Shall free the earth from never-ceasing fear.
He shall receive the life of gods, and see
Heroes with gods commingling, and himself
Be seen of them, and with his father's worth
Reign o'er a world at peace. For thee, O boy,
First shall the earth, untilled, pour freely forth
Her childish gifts, the gadding ivy-spray
With foxglove and Egyptian bean-flower mixed,
And laughing-eyed acanthus. Of themselves,
Untended, will the she-goats then bring home
Their udders swollen with milk, while flocks afield
Shall of the monstrous lion have no fear.
Thy very cradle shall pour forth for thee
Caressing flowers. The serpent too shall die,
Die shall the treacherous poison-plant, and far
And wide Assyrian spices spring. But soon
As thou hast skill to read of heroes' fame,
And of thy father's deeds, and inly learn
What virtue is, the plain by slow degrees
With waving corn-crops shall to golden grow,
From the wild briar shall hang the blushing grape,
And stubborn oaks sweat honey-dew. Nathless
Yet shall there lurk within of ancient wrong
Some traces, bidding tempt the deep with ships,
Gird towns with walls, with furrows cleave the earth.
Therewith a second Tiphys shall there be,
Her hero-freight a second Argo bear;
New wars too shall arise, and once again
Some great Achilles to some Troy be sent.
Then, when the mellowing years have made thee man,
No more shall mariner sail, nor pine-tree bark
Ply traffic on the sea, but every land

Shall all things bear alike: the glebe no more
Shall feel the harrow's grip, nor vine the hook;
The sturdy ploughman shall loose yoke from steer,
Nor wool with varying colours learn to lie;
But in the meadows shall the ram himself,
Now with soft flush of purple, now with tint
Of yellow saffron, teach his fleece to shine.
While clothed in natural scarlet graze the lambs.
"Such still, such ages weave ye, as ye run,"
Sang to their spindles the consenting Fates
By Destiny's unalterable decree.
Assume thy greatness, for the time draws nigh,
Dear child of gods, great progeny of Jove!
See how it totters- the world's orbed might,
Earth, and wide ocean, and the vault profound,
All, see, enraptured of the coming time!
Ah! might such length of days to me be given,
And breath suffice me to rehearse thy deeds,
Nor Thracian Orpheus should out-sing me then,
Nor Linus, though his mother this, and that
His sire should aid- Orpheus Calliope,
And Linus fair Apollo. Nay, though Pan,
With Arcady for judge, my claim contest,
With Arcady for judge great Pan himself
Should own him foiled, and from the field retire.

Begin to greet thy mother with a smile,
O baby-boy! ten months of weariness
For thee she bore: O baby-boy, begin!
For him, on whom his parents have not smiled,
Gods deem not worthy of their board or bed.

ECLOGUE V

MENALCAS , MOPSUS

MENALCAS
Why, Mopsus, being both together met,
You skilled to breathe upon the slender reeds,
I to sing ditties, do we not sit down
Here where the elm-trees and the hazels blend?

MOPSUS
You are the elder, 'tis for me to bide
Your choice, Menalcas, whether now we seek
Yon shade that quivers to the changeful breeze,
Or the cave's shelter. Look you how the cave
Is with the wild vine's clusters over-laced!

MENALCAS
None but Amyntas on these hills of ours
Can vie with you.

MOPSUS
What if he also strive
To out-sing Phoebus?

MENALCAS
Do you first begin,
Good Mopsus, whether minded to sing aught
Of Phyllis and her loves, or Alcon's praise,
Or to fling taunts at Codrus. Come, begin,
While Tityrus watches o'er the grazing kids.

MOPSUS
Nay, then, I will essay what late I carved
On a green beech-tree's rind, playing by turns,
And marking down the notes; then afterward
Bid you Amyntas match them if he can

MENALCAS
As limber willow to pale olive yields,
As lowly Celtic nard to rose-buds bright,
So, to my mind, Amyntas yields to you.
But hold awhile, for to the cave we come.

MOPSUS

"For Daphnis cruelly slain wept all the Nymphs-
Ye hazels, bear them witness, and ye streams-
When she, his mother, clasping in her arms
The hapless body of the son she bare,
To gods and stars unpitying, poured her plaint.
Then, Daphnis, to the cooling streams were none
That drove the pastured oxen, then no beast
Drank of the river, or would the grass-blade touch.
Nay, the wild rocks and woods then voiced the roar
Of Afric lions mourning for thy death.
Daphnis, 'twas thou bad'st yoke to Bacchus' car
Armenian tigresses, lead on the pomp
Of revellers, and with tender foliage wreathe
The bending spear-wands. As to trees the vine
Is crown of glory, as to vines the grape,
Bulls to the herd, to fruitful fields the corn,
So the one glory of thine own art thou.
When the Fates took thee hence, then Pales' self,
And even Apollo, left the country lone.
Where the plump barley-grain so oft we sowed,
There but wild oats and barren darnel spring;
For tender violet and narcissus bright
Thistle and prickly thorn uprear their heads.
Now, O ye shepherds, strew the ground with leaves,
And o'er the fountains draw a shady veil-
So Daphnis to his memory bids be done-
And rear a tomb, and write thereon this verse:
'I, Daphnis in the woods, from hence in fame
Am to the stars exalted, guardian once
Of a fair flock, myself more fair than they.'"

MENALCAS

So is thy song to me, poet divine,
As slumber on the grass to weary limbs,
Or to slake thirst from some sweet-bubbling rill
In summer's heat. Nor on the reeds alone,
But with thy voice art thou, thrice happy boy,
Ranked with thy master, second but to him.
Yet will I, too, in turn, as best I may,
Sing thee a song, and to the stars uplift
Thy Daphnis- Daphnis to the stars extol,
For me too Daphnis loved.

MOPSUS

Than such a boon
What dearer could I deem? the boy himself
Was worthy to be sung, and many a time
Hath Stimichon to me your singing praised.

MENALCAS

"In dazzling sheen with unaccustomed eyes
Daphnis stands rapt before Olympus' gate,
And sees beneath his feet the clouds and stars.
Wherefore the woods and fields, Pan, shepherd-folk,
And Dryad-maidens, thrill with eager joy;
Nor wolf with treacherous wile assails the flock,
Nor nets the stag: kind Daphnis loveth peace.
The unshorn mountains to the stars up-toss
Voices of gladness; ay, the very rocks,
The very thickets, shout and sing, 'A god,
A god is he, Menalcas "Be thou kind,
Propitious to thine own. Lo! altars four,
Twain to thee, Daphnis, and to Phoebus twain
For sacrifice, we build; and I for thee
Two beakers yearly of fresh milk afoam,
And of rich olive-oil two bowls, will set;
And of the wine-god's bounty above all,
If cold, before the hearth, or in the shade
At harvest-time, to glad the festal hour,
From flasks of Ariusian grape will pour
Sweet nectar. Therewithal at my behest
Shall Lyctian Aegon and Damoetas sing,
And Alphesiboeus emulate in dance
The dancing Satyrs. This, thy service due,
Shalt thou lack never, both when we pay the Nymphs
Our yearly vows, and when with lustral rites
The fields we hallow. Long as the wild boar
Shall love the mountain-heights, and fish the streams,
While bees on thyme and crickets feed on dew,
Thy name, thy praise, thine honour, shall endure.
Even as to Bacchus and to Ceres, so
To thee the swain his yearly vows shall make;
And thou thereof, like them, shalt quittance claim."

MOPSUS

How, how repay thee for a song so rare?
For not the whispering south-wind on its way
So much delights me, nor wave-smitten beach,
Nor streams that race adown their bouldered beds.

MENALCAS

First this frail hemlock-stalk to you I give,
Which taught me "Corydon with love was fired
For fair Alexis," ay, and this beside,
"Who owns the flock?- Meliboeus?"

MOPSUS

But take you
This shepherd's crook, which, howso hard he begged,
Antigenes, then worthy to be loved,
Prevailed not to obtain- with brass, you see,
And equal knots, Menalcas, fashioned fair!

ECLOGUE VI

TO VARUS

First my Thalia stooped in sportive mood
To Syracusan strains, nor blushed within
The woods to house her. When I sought to tell
Of battles and of kings, the Cynthian god
Plucked at mine ear and warned me: "Tityrus,
Beseems a shepherd-wight to feed fat sheep,
But sing a slender song." Now, Varus, I-
For lack there will not who would laud thy deeds,
And treat of dolorous wars- will rather tune
To the slim oaten reed my silvan lay.
I sing but as vouchsafed me; yet even this
If, if but one with ravished eyes should read,
Of thee, O Varus, shall our tamarisks
And all the woodland ring; nor can there be
A page more dear to Phoebus, than the page
Where, foremost writ, the name of Varus stands.

Speed ye, Pierian Maids! Within a cave
Young Chromis and Mnasyllos chanced to see
Silenus sleeping, flushed, as was his wont,
With wine of yesterday. Not far aloof,
Slipped from his head, the garlands lay, and there
By its worn handle hung a ponderous cup.
Approaching- for the old man many a time
Had balked them both of a long hoped-for song-
Garlands to fetters turned, they bind him fast.
Then Aegle, fairest of the Naiad-band,
Aegle came up to the half-frightened boys,
Came, and, as now with open eyes he lay,
With juice of blood-red mulberries smeared him o'er,
Both brow and temples. Laughing at their guile,
And crying, "Why tie the fetters? loose me, boys;
Enough for you to think you had the power;
Now list the songs you wish for- songs for you,
Another meed for her" -forthwith began.
Then might you see the wild things of the wood,
With Fauns in sportive frolic beat the time,
And stubborn oaks their branchy summits bow.
Not Phoebus doth the rude Parnassian crag
So ravish, nor Orpheus so entrance the heights
Of Rhodope or Ismarus: for he sang
How through the mighty void the seeds were driven
Of earth, air, ocean, and of liquid fire,
How all that is from these beginnings grew,
And the young world itself took solid shape,
Then 'gan its crust to harden, and in the deep
Shut Nereus off, and mould the forms of things
Little by little; and how the earth amazed
Beheld the new sun shining, and the showers
Fall, as the clouds soared higher, what time the woods

'Gan first to rise, and living things to roam
Scattered among the hills that knew them not.
Then sang he of the stones by Pyrrha cast,
Of Saturn's reign, and of Prometheus' theft,
And the Caucasian birds, and told withal
Nigh to what fountain by his comrades left
The mariners cried on Hylas till the shore
"Then Re-echoed "Hylas, Hylas! soothed
Pasiphae with the love of her white bull-
Happy if cattle-kind had never been!-
O ill-starred maid, what frenzy caught thy soul
The daughters too of Proetus filled the fields
With their feigned lowings, yet no one of them
Of such unhallowed union e'er was fain
As with a beast to mate, though many a time
On her smooth forehead she had sought for horns,
And for her neck had feared the galling plough.
O ill-starred maid! thou roamest now the hills,
While on soft hyacinths he, his snowy side
Reposing, under some dark ilex now
Chews the pale herbage, or some heifer tracks
Amid the crowding herd. Now close, ye Nymphs,
Ye Nymphs of Dicte, close the forest-glades,
If haply there may chance upon mine eyes
The white bull's wandering foot-prints: him belike
Following the herd, or by green pasture lured,
Some kine may guide to the Gortynian stalls.
Then sings he of the maid so wonder-struck
With the apples of the Hesperids, and then
With moss-bound, bitter bark rings round the forms
Of Phaethon's fair sisters, from the ground
Up-towering into poplars. Next he sings
Of Gallus wandering by Permessus' stream,
And by a sister of the Muses led
To the Aonian mountains, and how all
The choir of Phoebus rose to greet him; how
The shepherd Linus, singer of songs divine,
Brow-bound with flowers and bitter parsley, spake:
"These reeds the Muses give thee, take them thou,
Erst to the aged bard of Ascra given,
Wherewith in singing he was wont to draw
Time-rooted ash-trees from the mountain heights.
With these the birth of the Grynean grove
Be voiced by thee, that of no grove beside
Apollo more may boast him." Wherefore speak
Of Scylla, child of Nisus, who, 'tis said,
Her fair white loins with barking monsters girt
Vexed the Dulichian ships, and, in the deep
Swift-eddying whirlpool, with her sea-dogs tore
The trembling mariners? or how he told
Of the changed limbs of Tereus- what a feast,
What gifts, to him by Philomel were given;
How swift she sought the desert, with what wings
Hovered in anguish o'er her ancient home?
All that, of old, Eurotas, happy stream,
Heard, as Apollo mused upon the lyre,
And bade his laurels learn, Silenus sang;
Till from Olympus, loth at his approach,
Vesper, advancing, bade the shepherds tell
Their tale of sheep, and pen them in the fold.

ECLOGUE VII

MELIBOEUS, CORYDON, THYRSIS

Daphnis beneath a rustling ilex-tree
Had sat him down; Thyrsis and Corydon
Had gathered in the flock, Thyrsis the sheep,
And Corydon the she-goats swollen with milk-
Both in the flower of age, Arcadians both,
Ready to sing, and in like strain reply.
Hither had strayed, while from the frost I fend
My tender myrtles, the he-goat himself,
Lord of the flock; when Daphnis I espy!
Soon as he saw me, "Hither haste," he cried,
"O Meliboeus! goat and kids are safe;
And, if you have an idle hour to spare,
Rest here beneath the shade. Hither the steers
Will through the meadows, of their own free will,
Untended come to drink. Here Mincius hath
With tender rushes rimmed his verdant banks,
And from yon sacred oak with busy hum
The bees are swarming." What was I to do?
No Phyllis or Alcippe left at home
Had I, to shelter my new-weaned lambs,
And no slight matter was a singing-bout
'Twixt Corydon and Thyrsis. Howsoe'er,
I let my business wait upon their sport.
So they began to sing, voice answering voice
In strains alternate- for alternate strains
The Muses then were minded to recall-
First Corydon, then Thyrsis in reply.

CORYDON
"Libethrian Nymphs, who are my heart's delight,
Grant me, as doth my Codrus, so to sing-
Next to Apollo he- or if to this
We may not all attain, my tuneful pipe
Here on this sacred pine shall silent hang."

THYRSIS
"Arcadian shepherds, wreathe with ivy-spray
Your budding poet, so that Codrus burst
With envy: if he praise beyond my due,
Then bind my brow with foxglove, lest his tongue
With evil omen blight the coming bard."

CORYDON
"This bristling boar's head, Delian Maid, to thee,
With branching antlers of a sprightly stag,
Young Micon offers: if his luck but hold,
Full-length in polished marble, ankle-bound
With purple buskin, shall thy statue stand."

THYRSIS
"A bowl of milk, Priapus, and these cakes,
Yearly, it is enough for thee to claim;
Thou art the guardian of a poor man's plot.
Wrought for a while in marble, if the flock
At lambing time be filled,stand there in gold."

CORYDON
"Daughter of Nereus, Galatea mine,
Sweeter than Hybla-thyme, more white than swans,
Fairer than ivy pale, soon as the steers
Shall from their pasture to the stalls repair,
If aught for Corydon thou carest, come."

THYRSIS
"Now may I seem more bitter to your taste
Than herb Sardinian, rougher than the broom,
More worthless than strewn sea-weed, if to-day
Hath not a year out-lasted! Fie for shame!
Go home, my cattle, from your grazing go!"

CORYDON
"Ye mossy springs, and grass more soft than sleep,
And arbute green with thin shade sheltering you,
Ward off the solstice from my flock, for now
Comes on the burning summer, now the buds
Upon the limber vine-shoot 'gin to swell."

THYRSIS
"Here is a hearth, and resinous logs, here fire
Unstinted, and doors black with ceaseless smoke.
Here heed we Boreas' icy breath as much
As the wolf heeds the number of the flock,
Or furious rivers their restraining banks."

CORYDON
"The junipers and prickly chestnuts stand,
And 'neath each tree lie strewn their several fruits,
Now the whole world is smiling, but if fair
Alexis from these hill-slopes should away,
Even the rivers you would ; see run dry."

THYRSIS
"The field is parched, the grass-blades thirst to death
In the faint air; Liber hath grudged the hills
His vine's o'er-shadowing: should my Phyllis come,
Green will be all the grove, and Jupiter
Descend in floods of fertilizing rain."

CORYDON
"The poplar doth Alcides hold most dear,
The vine Iacchus, Phoebus his own bays,
And Venus fair the myrtle: therewithal
Phyllis doth hazels love, and while she loves,
Myrtle nor bay the hazel shall out-vie."

THYRSIS
"Ash in the forest is most beautiful,
Pine in the garden, poplar by the stream,
Fir on the mountain-height; but if more oft
Thou'ldst come to me, fair Lycidas, to thee
Both forest-ash, and garden-pine should bow."

MELIBOEUS
These I remember, and how Thyrsis strove
For victory in vain. From that time forth
Is Corydon still Corydon with us.

ECLOGUE VIII

TO POLLIO, DAMON, ALPHESIBOEUS

Of Damon and Alphesiboeus now,
Those shepherd-singers at whose rival strains
The heifer wondering forgot to graze,
The lynx stood awe-struck, and the flowing streams,
Unwonted loiterers, stayed their course to hear-
How Damon and Alphesiboeus sang
Their pastoral ditties, will I tell the tale.

Thou, whether broad Timavus' rocky banks
Thou now art passing, or dost skirt the shore
Of the Illyrian main,- will ever dawn
That day when I thy deeds may celebrate,
Ever that day when through the whole wide world
I may renown thy verse- that verse alone
Of Sophoclean buskin worthy found?
With thee began, to thee shall end, the strain.
Take thou these songs that owe their birth to thee,
And deign around thy temples to let creep
This ivy-chaplet 'twixt the conquering bays.

Scarce had night's chilly shade forsook the sky
What time to nibbling sheep the dewy grass
Tastes sweetest, when, on his smooth shepherd-staff
Of olive leaning, Damon thus began.

DAMON
"Rise, Lucifer, and, heralding the light,
Bring in the genial day, while I make moan
Fooled by vain passion for a faithless bride,
For Nysa, and with this my dying breath
Call on the gods, though little it bestead-
The gods who heard her vows and heeded not.

"Begin, my flute, with me Maenalian lays.
Ever hath Maenalus his murmuring groves
And whispering pines, and ever hears the songs
Of love-lorn shepherds, and of Pan, who first
Brooked not the tuneful reed should idle lie.

"Begin, my flute, with me Maenalian lays.
Nysa to Mopsus given! what may not then
We lovers look for? soon shall we see mate
Griffins with mares, and in the coming age
Shy deer and hounds together come to drink.

"Begin, my flute, with me Maenalian lays.
Now, Mopsus, cut new torches, for they bring
Your bride along; now, bridegroom, scatter nuts:
Forsaking Oeta mounts the evening star!

"Begin, my flute, with me Maenalian lays.
O worthy of thy mate, while all men else
Thou scornest, and with loathing dost behold
My shepherd's pipe, my goats, my shaggy brow,
And untrimmed beard, nor deem'st that any god
For mortal doings hath regard or care.

"Begin, my flute, with me Maenalian lays.
Once with your mother, in our orchard-garth,
A little maid I saw you- I your guide-
Plucking the dewy apples. My twelfth year
I scarce had entered, and could barely reach
The brittle boughs. I looked, and I was lost;
A sudden frenzy swept my wits away.

"Begin, my flute, with me Maenalian lays.
Now know I what Love is: 'mid savage rocks
Tmaros or Rhodope brought forth the boy,
Or Garamantes in earth's utmost bounds-
No kin of ours, nor of our blood begot.

"Begin, my flute, with me Maenalian lays.
Fierce Love it was once steeled a mother's heart
With her own offspring's blood her hands to imbrue:
Mother, thou too wert cruel; say wert thou
More cruel, mother, or more ruthless he?
Ruthless the boy, thou, mother, cruel too.

"Begin, my flute, with me Maenalian lays.
Now let the wolf turn tail and fly the sheep,
Tough oaks bear golden apples, alder-trees
Bloom with narcissus-flower, the tamarisk
Sweat with rich amber, and the screech-owl vie
In singing with the swan: let Tityrus
Be Orpheus, Orpheus in the forest-glade,
Arion 'mid his dolphins on the deep.

"Begin, my flute, with me Maenalian lays.
Yea, be the whole earth to mid-ocean turned!
Farewell, ye woodlands I from the tall peak
Of yon aerial rock will headlong plunge
Into the billows: this my latest gift,
From dying lips bequeathed thee, see thou keep.
Cease now, my flute, now cease Maenalian lays."

Thus Damon: but do ye, Pierian Maids-
We cannot all do all things- tell me how
Alphesiboeus to his strain replied.

ALPHESIBOEUS
"Bring water, and with soft wool-fillet bind
These altars round about, and burn thereon
Rich vervain and male frankincense, that I
May strive with magic spells to turn astray
My lover's saner senses, whereunto
There lacketh nothing save the power of song.

"Draw from the town, my songs, draw Daphnis home.
Songs can the very moon draw down from heaven
Circe with singing changed from human form
The comrades of Ulysses, and by song
Is the cold meadow-snake, asunder burst.

"Draw from the town, my songs, draw Daphnis home.
These triple threads of threefold colour first
I twine about thee, and three times withal
Around these altars do thine image bear:
Uneven numbers are the god's delight.

"Draw from the town, my songs, draw Daphnis home.
Now, Amaryllis, ply in triple knots
The threefold colours; ply them fast, and say
This is the chain of Venus that I ply.

"Draw from the town, my songs, draw Daphnis home.
As by the kindling of the self-same fire
Harder this clay, this wax the softer grows,
So by my love may Daphnis; sprinkle meal,
And with bitumen burn the brittle bays.
Me Daphnis with his cruelty doth burn,
I to melt cruel Daphnis burn this bay.

"Draw from the town, my songs, draw Daphnis home.
As when some heifer, seeking for her steer
Through woodland and deep grove, sinks wearied out
On the green sedge beside a stream, love-lorn,
Nor marks the gathering night that calls her home-
As pines that heifer, with such love as hers
May Daphnis pine, and I not care to heal.

"Draw from the town, my songs, draw Daphnis home.
These relics once, dear pledges of himself,
The traitor left me, which, O earth, to thee
Here on this very threshold I commit-
Pledges that bind him to redeem the debt.

"Draw from the town, my songs, draw Daphnis home.
These herbs of bane to me did Moeris give,
In Pontus culled, where baneful herbs abound.
With these full oft have I seen Moeris change
To a wolf's form, and hide him in the woods,
Oft summon spirits from the tomb's recess,
And to new fields transport the standing corn.

"Draw from the town, my songs, draw Daphnis home.
Take ashes, Amaryllis, fetch them forth,
And o'er your head into the running brook
Fling them, nor look behind: with these will
Upon the heart of Daphnis make essay.
Nothing for gods, nothing for songs cares he.

"Draw from the town, my songs, draw Daphnis home.
Look, look I the very embers of themselves
Have caught the altar with a flickering flame,
While I delay to fetch them: may the sign
Prove lucky! something it must mean, for sure,
And Hylax on the threshold 'gins to bark!
May we believe it, or are lovers still
By their own fancies fooled?

Give o'er, my songs,
Daphnis is coming from the town, give o'er."

ECLOGUE IX

LYCIDAS, MOERIS

LYCIDAS
Say whither, Moeris?- Make you for the town,
Or on what errand bent?

MOERIS
O Lycidas,
We have lived to see, what never yet we feared,
An interloper own our little farm,
And say, "Be off, you former husbandmen!
These fields are mine." Now, cowed and out of heart,
Since Fortune turns the whole world upside down,
We are taking him- ill luck go with the same!-'
These kids you see.

LYCIDAS
But surely I had heard
That where the hills first draw from off the plain,
And the high ridge with gentle slope descends,
Down to the brook-side and the broken crests
Of yonder veteran beeches, all the land
Was by the songs of your Menalcas saved.

MOERIS
Heard it you had, and so the rumour ran,
But 'mid the clash of arms, my Lycidas,
Our songs avail no more than, as 'tis said,
Doves of Dodona when an eagle comes.
Nay, had I not, from hollow ilex-bole
Warned by a raven on the left, cut short
The rising feud, nor I, your Moeris here,
No, nor Menalcas, were alive to-day.

LYCIDAS
Alack! could any of so foul a crime
Be guilty? Ah! how nearly, thyself,
Reft was the solace that we had in thee,
Menalcas! Who then of the Nymphs had sung,
Or who with flowering herbs bestrewn the ground,
And o'er the fountains drawn a leafy veil?-
Who sung the stave I filched from you that day
To Amaryllis wending, our hearts' joy?-
"While I am gone, 'tis but a little way,
Feed, Tityrus, my goats, and, having fed,
Drive to the drinking-pool, and, as you drive,
Beware the he-goat; with his horn he butts."

MOERIS

Ay, or to Varus that half-finished lay,
"Varus, thy name, so still our Mantua live-
Mantua to poor Cremona all too near-
Shall singing swans bear upward to the stars."

LYCIDAS

So may your swarms Cyrnean yew-trees shun,
Your kine with cytisus their udders swell,
Begin, if aught you have. The Muses made
Me too a singer; I too have sung; the swains
Call me a poet, but I believe them not:
For naught of mine, or worthy Varius yet
Or Cinna deem I, but account myself
A cackling goose among melodious swans.

MOERIS

'Twas in my thought to do so, Lycidas;
Even now was I revolving silently
If this I could recall- no paltry song:
"Come, Galatea, what pleasure is 't to play
Amid the waves? Here glows the Spring, here earth
Beside the streams pours forth a thousand flowers;
Here the white poplar bends above the cave,
And the lithe vine weaves shadowy covert: come,
Leave the mad waves to beat upon the shore."

LYCIDAS

What of the strain I heard you singing once
On a clear night alone? the notes I still
Remember, could I but recall the words.

MOERIS

"Why, Daphnis, upward gazing, do you mark
The ancient risings of the Signs? for look
Where Dionean Caesar's star comes forth
In heaven, to gladden all the fields with corn,
And to the grape upon the sunny slopes
Her colour bring! Now, the pears;
So shall your children's children pluck their fruit.

Time carries all things, even our wits, away.
Oft, as a boy, I sang the sun to rest,
But all those songs are from my memory fled,
And even his voice is failing Moeris now;
The wolves eyed Moeris first: but at your wish
Menalcas will repeat them oft enow.

LYCIDAS

Your pleas but linger out my heart's desire:
Now all the deep is into silence hushed,
And all the murmuring breezes sunk to sleep.
We are half-way thither, for Bianor's tomb
Begins to show: here, Moeris, where the hinds
Are lopping the thick leafage, let us sing.
Set down the kids, yet shall we reach the town;
Or, if we fear the night may gather rain
Ere we arrive, then singing let us go,
Our way to lighten; and, that we may thus
Go singing, I will case you of this load.

MOERIS
Cease, boy, and get we to the work in hand:
We shall sing better when himself is come.

ECLOGUE X

GALLUS

This now, the very latest of my toils,
Vouchsafe me, Arethusa! needs must I
Sing a brief song to Gallus- brief, but yet
Such as Lycoris' self may fitly read.
Who would not sing for Gallus? So, when thou
Beneath Sicanian billows glidest on,
May Doris blend no bitter wave with thine,
Begin! The love of Gallus be our theme,
And the shrewd pangs he suffered, while, hard by,
The flat-nosed she-goats browse the tender brush.
We sing not to deaf ears; no word of ours
But the woods echo it. What groves or lawns
Held you, ye Dryad-maidens, when for love-
Love all unworthy of a loss so dear-
Gallus lay dying? for neither did the slopes
Of Pindus or Parnassus stay you then,
No, nor Aonian Aganippe. Him
Even the laurels and the tamarisks wept;
For him, outstretched beneath a lonely rock,
Wept pine-clad Maenalus, and the flinty crags
Of cold Lycaeus. The sheep too stood around-
Of us they feel no shame, poet divine;
Nor of the flock be thou ashamed: even fair
Adonis by the rivers fed his sheep-
Came shepherd too, and swine-herd footing slow,
And, from the winter-acorns dripping-wet
Menalcas. All with one accord exclaim:
"From whence this love of thine?" Apollo came;
"Gallus, art mad?" he cried, "thy bosom's care
Another love is following."Therewithal
Silvanus came, with rural honours crowned;
The flowering fennels and tall lilies shook
Before him. Yea, and our own eyes beheld
Pan, god of Arcady, with blood-red juice
Of the elder-berry, and with vermilion, dyed.
"Wilt ever make an end?" quoth he, "behold
Love recks not aught of it: his heart no more
With tears is sated than with streams the grass,
Bees with the cytisus, or goats with leaves."
"Yet will ye sing, Arcadians, of my woes
Upon your mountains," sadly he replied-
"Arcadians, that alone have skill to sing.
O then how softly would my ashes rest,
If of my love, one day, your flutes should tell!
And would that I, of your own fellowship,
Or dresser of the ripening grape had been,
Or guardian of the flock! for surely then,
Let Phyllis, or Amyntas, or who else,
Bewitch me- what if swart Amyntas be?
Dark is the violet, dark the hyacinth-

Among the willows, 'neath the limber vine,
Reclining would my love have lain with me,
Phyllis plucked garlands, or Amyntas sung.
Here are cool springs, soft mead and grove, Lycoris;
Here might our lives with time have worn away.
But me mad love of the stern war-god holds
Armed amid weapons and opposing foes.
Whilst thou- Ah! might I but believe it not!-
Alone without me, and from home afar,
Look'st upon Alpine snows and frozen Rhine.
Ah! may the frost not hurt thee, may the sharp
And jagged ice not wound thy tender feet!
I will depart, re-tune the songs I framed
In verse Chalcidian to the oaten reed
Of the Sicilian swain. Resolved am I
In the woods, rather, with wild beasts to couch,
And bear my doom, and character my love
Upon the tender tree-trunks: they will grow,
And you, my love, grow with them. And meanwhile
I with the Nymphs will haunt Mount Maenalus,
Or hunt the keen wild boar. No frost so cold
But I will hem with hounds thy forest-glades,
Parthenius. Even now, methinks, I range
O'er rocks, through echoing groves, and joy to launch
Cydonian arrows from a Parthian bow.-
As if my madness could find healing thus,
Or that god soften at a mortal's grief!
Now neither Hamadryads, no, nor songs
Delight me more: ye woods, away with you!
No pangs of ours can change him; not though we
In the mid-frost should drink of Hebrus' stream,
And in wet winters face Sithonian snows,
Or, when the bark of the tall elm-tree bole
Of drought is dying, should, under Cancer's Sign,
In Aethiopian deserts drive our flocks.
Love conquers all things; yield we too to love!"

These songs, Pierian Maids, shall it suffice
Your poet to have sung, the while he sat,
And of slim mallow wove a basket fine:
To Gallus ye will magnify their worth,
Gallus, for whom my love grows hour by hour,
As the green alder shoots in early Spring.
Come, let us rise: the shade is wont to be
Baneful to singers; baneful is the shade
Cast by the juniper, crops sicken too
In shade. Now homeward, having fed your fill--
Eve's star is rising-go, my she-goats, go.

www.ingramcontent.com/pod-product-compliance
Lightning Source LLC
LaVergne TN
LVHW050950080826
845145LV00004B/1458

9781988297439